starting with the "New deal."

The liberals were able to get enough power to sling off the bridle that had controlled them since the founding of the country. How they slung off the bridle was by eliminating a free floating wage scale in America. It doesn't matter how low, if it's not free floating it is death to a free market economy. You see, a free floating wage and price scale is the foundation of a free market place system.

By enacting the new deal "Minimum wage law" it prevents wages and prices from free floating and staying in balance with each other. That have allowed liberals to tax and spend to kingdom come. A free floating wage scale won't let the cost of living (prices) go above what the majority poor can afford. Then like throughout history the poor under a nuclear family umbrella can pay their own food and doctor bills.

That is why as long as liberals are unbridled because of the "Minimum wage law" you can forget about ever saving the USA. There is no stopping the liberals from self destructing this nation out of existence.

If the "Minimum wage law" is not abolished to bridle the liberals back under control we all might as well kiss individual freedom and the good Ole USA goodbye forever. **SIRMANS LOG: 17 OCTOBER 2013, 0148 HOURS**

DEBT SO DEEP THE USA GOODS WILL BE SOLD OFF LIKE A HOOKER'S ON THE STREETS!

To all of the masses that don't understand the destruction the "Minimum wage law" has done to the USA, I'm still trying to get through your thick scull. Practical all of the foundation and infrastructure of the USA were built before the minimum wage law of the "Fair labor standards act of 1938."

Most of the bridges and water and sewage systems in major cities throughout the USA were built before a minimum wage law. Now, throughout the USA practically everything is beginning to fall apart. And I'm here to tell you there is no way in hell these infrastructures are going to be replaces with a minimum wage law in place.

There is no mystery about it the fact is no free market economy can support this liberal installed provider welfare state, it can barely support a proper military. All throughout history without a minimum wage law the people were able to provide for themselves and support a government, too. But, the minimum wage law prevents that; it won't let

Liberalism Dissected, Discovered To Be Bane To Freedom

Sure, I am trying to dissect the liberal psyche but only to try to understand them. I am in awe of liberals, as a group they are smarter, more intelligent, and above average. And they are super aggressive, why do you think they have taken over and control the whole education system and almost every institution in America. Hardcore liberals make up only about 20 percent of the entire population, so how can this be.

Liberalism is why it is almost impossible for a nation to remain free because as a rule hardcore liberals tend not to adhere to any internal restraints like high morals. You can't think of nothing liberals won't do to gain and keep power. You couple that with a useless negative anti-survivalist mainstream news media, and that is why liberals can get away with practically anything.

There must be physical barriers to bridle them, like a no minimum wage law. When they get enough power to remove a physical barrier it is only a matter of time before they make it impossible for freedom to exist.

The further any nation get away from a free market place the poorer it will get. The liberals are in almost total control of the USA now and only getting rid of the minimum wage will restore a physical barrier.

Otherwise, like a junkie on the street trying to get a fix, their fix is to tax and spend to kingdom come.

I am going to compare liberalism to the phenomenon of greed. On the surface most people think greed is a bad thing, but it is not. A successful capitalist system cannot work unless there is an abundance of greed. Like electricity greed is very dangerous but there is no greater energy packed motivating force in our entire human make up than greed.

The trick is to be able to harness greed, but never severely restrict it, that is why pure communism and socialism will always fail. A free market place with unrestricted competition will harness greed without restricting it's ability to produce almost unlimited amounts of abundance. Harnessed greed is what made the USA the greatest and richest nation to ever exist.

I said I would compare liberals to the phenomenon of greed. So, I will make the comparison, like electricity and greed, unbridled liberalism is dangerous that is why the USA has spent itself almost out of existence. Again, with liberals we have the most aggressive, smartest, and intelligent people on earth. But, here is what happened

Liberalism Dissected, Discovered To Be Bane To Freedom

ONLY BRIDLING LIBERALS WILL STOP THEIR TAX AND SPEND MADNESS!

GREAT WRITER FREDDIE L SIRMANS, SR. DISSECTS LIBERALISM AND DISCOVERS WHY LIBERALISM IS PRONE TO SELF-DESTRUCT WHATEVER IT TOUCHES.

OK folks, concerning the shutdown, I'm going to give you the truth the whole truth and nothing but the truth. The liberals are spouting the "Big lie" like it's an established fact that the republicans caused the shutdown of the government.

Hogwash, no one side shut down the government, two uncompromising schools of thought shut down the government. In fact I agree with the intentions of the hard core conservative republicans, but, I totally disagree with their action in this case.

I knew they didn't have a snowball chance in hell of succeeding. Let's examine the liberal mentality in America: In my view the liberal mentality has all but destroyed this great nation of individual freedom. We are all good Americans, and I love liberals and all people. But, there is nothing innate about being a liberal.

Many a liberals have changed from being a liberal over night after being slammed upside the head and robbed of all of their possessions. That drastic experience caused them to see the light. I think liberalism results from a lack of survival awareness, which makes them shallow.

This is just my one man opinion and nothing else; I just think someone shallow with a weak survival instinct having power can be a dangerous thing. You see, liberals see people losing jobs, can't pay their bills, and suffering all around.

The first thing a liberal will think or do is look for something or somebody to blame. Never in a million years will a liberal realize it is he and his liberal policies that have shaped America ever since the "New deal." Benjamin Franklin said, "We have a republic if we can keep it."

Liberalism tends not to come from struggling or discipline households. But, now with our welfare state almost all you see coming from poor households is corrupted character and liberalism, who can trust the poor to work in their home now-a-days. However, this would be a cold and cruel world without liberals trying to make it safe for Bamba and for all, I love them.

the cost of living (prices) drop down enough for the majority poor to pay out of pocket for their own food and medical bills.

The government drives prices higher and higher by giving out free money on an individual basis thereby driving prices out of reach for everyone. Sure, the poor needs help, but the way to do that is for the government to run it own commissaries, housing, and clinics for the poor and use tokens or script for those who qualify, not contaminate the whole national economy for everyone, sheer madness.

The minimum wage law red tape also prevents bartering and people to people hiring. The shallow simple minded see the minimum wage only in terms of how much one make in wages, but that is just a facade. Forcing a minimum wage law on a free market economy is like pouring sugar in a gas tank, it gums up the works.

That is what is happening to the USA economy. The inner works are gummed up and we will continue going deeper and deeper into debt until the country's goods will be sold off like a hooker's on the streets. Sure, I'm giving a harsh bleak future outlook that will not be believed by the simple minded, but if the minimum wage law is not abolished that is exactly what is going to happen to the USA.

God save the USA. **SIRMANS LOG: 05 NOVEMBER 2013, 1343 HOURS**

A FINAL USA ASSESSMENT BEFORE DOOM!
Folks, here is my final assessment of the future of the USA before our economy collapse into total doom due to Obamacare. Fact one the liberals and democrats are hell bent on going socialist, communist, or authoritarian of some sort.

I believe these two groups are in denial, fantasy land, and totally ignorant of cause and effect. And if not for pain and hunger would deny reality itself. All they know is to tax and spend until kingdom come, this great nation is doomed for sure if they can't be defeated at the polls.

Now, on the other hand, fact two the conservatives and republicans offer the only possible hope of saving the USA from total doom. At least these two groups understand cause and effect and are not in total denial. But, remember I said hope, because that is about all these two groups has to offer.

The cold raw fact is the conservatives and

republicans don't know how to save the USA. They make the biggest mistake of all by thinking they can save the USA by cutting spending. Sure, it is true over spending is the problem and is what got the USA in this dire fix.

But, what all of this insane over spending has done is create a welfare state with masses upon masses of big government dependents. And these masses of dependents is the source of the Lib's and Dem's power, and opposition spending cuts just cements them in deeper. Plus, all cutting spending does is create a smaller welfare state pie that still must be divided as before, which will not save the country.

Political speaking overall spending cuts will keep the Democrats in power and republicans out of power and the country will be the loser. The solution for saving the USA and individual freedom is to dismantle the welfare state that the liberals and democrats have built, but even that can't be done political without cementing them deeper into power.

The problem is when the republicans do get their chance will they do what must be done; abolish the "Minimum wage law." I have preached and preached to no end the only solution, still no one want to hear it.

Liberalism Dissected, Discovered To Be Bane To Freedom

All is necessary to save our freedom and this great nation is to abolish the "Minimum wage law," period. Then the free market place and the process of natural selection will take it from there and save this great nation, there is no other way. It won't be easy but it is the only fighting chance we have left to save the USA and individual freedom.

Going this route will untie the free market place and then there will be jobs for all. It will also drop the cost of living where everyone will be able to pay out of pocket for their own food and doctor bills with the aid of the nuclear family.

Even neighbors will be able to hire neighbors and entrepreneurs will be untied to fill all of the nations needs like in days of old. However, government will still need to provide for the very poor and needy by setting up government run commissaries, housing, and clinics.

And there must be a use of token or script for all who qualify to prevent diluting and contamination the national free market economy. I am under no illusion I'm only telling you what it will take for the USA to survive, I know the powerful money people would rather go down with the ship they will never accept something of this sort.

So folks, that is it in a nut shell this is the only way the USA has a fighting chance to survive, I bid us farewell. **SIRMANS LOG: 31 OCTOBER 2013, 1354 HOURS**

DEMOCRAT PARTY MAY SPLIT INTO TWO FACTIONS OVER OBAMACARE!

One thing these wanna-be socialist and communist in the USA has yet to learn is you can't get what you really want except by Violent ruthless brute force and that ain't gonna happen in the USA, yet. In my view that is what this Obamacare so-called debacle actually boils down to.

The Supreme Court caved and allowed the liberals to get away with this usurp of freedom. But, authoritarian strong-arm tactics is not the American way. The USA is the freest country to ever exist and is beginning to figure out who are the real villains, here.

Forcing healthy young men and women to buy health insurance that they neither want nor need doesn't have anything to do with paying taxes. That is false reasoning, UN-American, and out right forced financial slavery, period. And the next step will be a writer like me disappearing in the middle of the night.

It is not about what flamboyant people with the gift of gab tells you, sure, pie in the sky promises sound good, but when the world all around you is crumbing how long will it take you to see the light. Of course some never will. Get a grip America. This whole Obamacare thing could split the Democrat party straight down the middle because there are some die-Hard's who will never yield one inch.

It's not panic time yet for the Dems, but this thing could blow wide open the flood gates.
SIRMANS LOG: 25 OCTOBER 2013, 1329 HOURS

OBAMACARE SIGNUP DEBACLE SLIGHT OF HAND!
Well, I'm one that doesn't buy this debacle for one second; I don't think it is an accident. And I will go even further and say they won't have a proper working model website until after the 2014 election. The liberals don't want the cold raw facts and cost to be known until they have hooked enough suckers that thinks it's free. I could go on and on but I think you get my drift.
SIRMANS LOG: 21 OCTOBER 2013, 1847 HOURS

IS IT TOO LATE FOR THE USA AND INDIVIDUAL FREEDOM TOO BE SAVED?

The fact is the anti-survival forces of culture rot and moral decay in the USA is even more deadly than a phony economy with irresponsible government spending. Even if the bills get paid the USA still can't survive unless the "Minimum wage law" is abolished now. Tomorrow may be too late.

That will save the USA economy and restore the nuclear family and get rid of culture rot and moral decay. No society can survive hard and troubled times without a strong nuclear and extended family system; there are no exceptions in history.

With a strong nuclear and extended family foundation civilization existed with trade and bartering for centuries, long before a currency (money) was invented. Again, a society can survive with or without money, but, no society can survive very long without a strong nuclear and extended family foundation. ours must be restored, now.
SIRMANS LOG: 15 OCTOBER 2013, 0953 HOURS

DO LIBERALS REALLY WANT MARTIAL LAW SO THEY CAN INSTALL FULL AUTHORITARIAN SOCIALIST RULE IN

AMERICA?
I believe the liberals are shooting for all of the marbles. I believe they want full martial law so they can install full authoritarian socialist rule in America. Maybe not all but I'm sure a lot of liberals would love a socialist state.

A full take over may seem out of the question, but, the way we are headed that is where it may end, something gotta give. I may have finally lost it, but this is my analysis.

SIRMANS LOG: 12 OCTOBER 2013, 1435 HOURS

STOP THE MADNESS; ABOLISH THE MINIMUM WAGE LAW NOW!
Why did the founding fathers to a man distrust democracy and made the great USA a republic? Well, in living color the proof of their wisdom is being proven here in the USA every day, but, totally ignored.

The USA today is mostly led by mob rule with the predominately liberal news media leading the charge. And their false God of political polling is their holy grail. When in history has the general public ever been right, almost never.

The general public is almost always uninformed, emotional, and easily led by those with the gift of gab and flamboyant personalities. This nation is on the brink of a total financial collapse and what the hell do the general public know, the liberal media sho-ain't informed them.

Where are the statesmen of today who will place the financial health of the nation above all else. The minimum wage law must go, please, somebody listen before it is too late.**SIRMANS LOG: 10 OCTOBER 2013, 2041 HOURS**

WE ALL ARE GOOD AMERICANS, BUT, MY BAD IF I THINK LIBERALS WITH POWER ARE SORT OF LIKE A KID BEHIND THE WHEEL, SORRY.
Please excuse me up front because I am fixing to rant. There is a reason why most of the world is poor and will always be poor. There is a reason why the USA was the richest nation ever, and have led the world in the most inventions and scientific break through's. But, 95 percent of today's USA population doesn't have a clue as to what made the USA so great.

Well, I'll tell you the reason, but first, starting with the "New deal" the liberals were able to grab enough power and with tax payers money buy off the voters with free goodies. And, for the first time they begin corrupting our culture. So, after years of corrupting our culture using the welfare state we are now reaping what the liberals sowed starting with the new deal. But, they could not have done it entirely alone.

Now, back to the two main reasons for what made the USA so great: The two major things that made the USA the greatest nation to ever exist were "Individual freedom and a genuine true "Free market place," minus a "Minimum wage law" villain. Let's face it concerning the stock market; the tail is now wagging the dog.

The USA government should never have gotten into the stock market, and the stock market should never have gotten into the government, enough said. Another thing, the government should never have become a social and family provider, it should have stayed with providing only for the military and a few other things the people couldn't do for themselves.

Now, masses upon masses of people are dependent on the government for their sole survival when it should be the other way around. You make government independent and it's going to take over, it already has the power. How profit affects government and our survival is one of the least understood things about our economy.

Government's sole survival depends on private business profit. After a point, the more government taxes business profit the less it is going to get. That is because fewer and fewer businesses will be able to make any profit to be taken.

The amount of profit USA private businesses can produce at the present is not enough to carry our welfare state load as it is, and then to add Obamacare is like adding another ton. That is insane, the economy can't help but collapse.

Here is the solution to our economic survival: First, abolish the "Minimum wage law" now. Next, all government spending must be separated from the national economy free market spending, because you can't have a free market with the infusion of mass amounts of government money distorting everything.

The only way to separate the two is for government to establish its own commissaries, housing, and clinics to care for the poor and needy. And use tokens or script for all who qualify. That will leave the national economy untainted and undistorted with inflation. Then the tax paying citizens won't have inflation with the cost of living out of sight.

The people will be able to pay for their own food and doctor bills. That will also allow the nuclear family to rebound. But, I must say I don't believe something sane with common sense like this is possible any more there are too few people with the wisdom and judgment left. We will just stay on course to sure doom.

Instead of creating "New deal" programs to aid the poor and needy men of real wisdom would never have destroyed the nuclear family system. All that is necessary to destroy the nuclear and extended family system is to take away a survival need for it, which the welfare state has done.

Now, when the USA and world economy collapse which won't be very long, we won't have a nuclear and extended family system strong enough to survive on. There is no telling how far civilization may regress backward, maybe all the way back to the Stone Age, and that is a fact. **SIRMANS LOG: 07 OCTOBER 2013, 1457 HOURS**

COMMUNICATION AND COMPROMISE IS THE FOUNDATION OF FREEDOM AND DEMOCRACY.

In a marriage or anything involving more than one person communication is key. The unwillingness to talk and communicate leaves only two options, force or separation, which neither is possible here. If they won't talk and communicate the people must demand it, period.

Besides, I understand how an economy works as well as anyone and I will repeat, the USA economy cannot swallow Obamacare and survive. And to all you doubting Thomas's that don't believe me; the proof should be forthcoming within a year.
SIRMANS LOG: 03 OCTOBER 2013, 2015 HOURS

IF REPUBLICANS ACTUALLY HOLD THEIR GROUND THE PUBLIC WILL DEMAND THE DEMS MAKE A SHUT-DOWN DEAL.
This is like high stakes poker! Sure, in a shut-down the first few days or so the republicans will be pounded fiercely with blame, but, the longer it goes the more the blame is going to shift to the Dems for not making a deal. After all this is not an authoritarian government, yet.

Some say cave now and save 2014, wrong, too late for that. No guts no glory, to cave now may guarantee a 2014 lost. There is no shame in going down swinging
SIRMANS LOG: 01 OCTOBER 2013, 1724 HOURS

F.L. SIRMANS WORDS OF FACT:

* Once the public believe the republicans are not going to cave they will shift blame to who is in charge and demand a shut-down deal.
* No business can survive and keep operating unless it makes a profit.
* All government income originates from private business profit, not from the tax payers.
* Government has no money or income unless it takes it directly or indirectly from private business profit.
* Profit is when an individual or a group of individuals has more possessions than necessary to maintain their own survival.
* No profit forthcoming, no one is going to extra produce except by force, then only enough to stay alive.
* It is impossible for the USA and individual freedom to be saved with a "Minimum wage law" in existence, because it is blocking the path to a true free market place.

* At this late stage only a genuine true "Free market Place" can save the USA and western civilization, and that is a given.

SIRMANS LOG: 30 SEPTEMBER 2013, 1216 HOURS

OBAMACARE FUNDING: OMG! DEMS THINK THEY ARE BIGGEST WINNERS, BUT ACTUALLY MAY BE THE DUMBEST

FOOLS!

The Obamacare mess is sort of like a high stakes poker game. But, I think the real hole cards are what the voting public is going to do in the 2014 and 2016 elections.

The Dems are praying for a government shutdown that will definitely give them an advantage going into these elections. And on the other hand there is a small group of gung-ho arch-conservatives that could care less if the government gets shut down in their effort to stop this funding.

Sure, everyone knows this small group of conservatives won't be able to stop this funding. Myself, I think their failure is a blessing in disguise. I think the worse possible nightmare may happen to the Dems if they go ahead and put Obamacare in effect at this time.

There is no risk to wait a year. It is already the law and nothing would really change, plus it would give them another year to get all of their ducks in line. And they would probably hold on to the senate.

That said, they are risking everything because the cold hard fact is the economy can't swallow Obamacare and unimaginable things are going to happen. The forty hour work week may be history. People may start losing jobs like crazy causing the dole to explode. And the tax base may start drastically dwindling.

With all that going on the voters may finally see the light and give the hated republicans their chance to shine in 2014 and 2016. If nothing else, this will give the Dems something to think about. **SIRMANS LOG: 24 SEPTEMBER 2013, 1948 HOURS**

ANY DRASTIC USA CUTS IN SPENDING WILL BE LIKE COMMITTING INSTANT ECONOMIC DEATH!
All of these decent good intention people that is hollering and demanding drastic cuts in government spending are economically ignorant.

To drastic cut spending in a welfare state before first abolishing the "Minimum wage law" is committing economic suicide. Drastic cuts in spending will only create a smaller welfare state pie, and it still will have to be divided as before with even more mouths to feed.

Starting with the "New deal" the shallow minded liberals brought us to this point, but, we all are guilty of taking the course of least resistance. Now, the end result is we are past the stage of no return. In my view there is no stopping it, the USA and world economy will soon collapse no matter what man does.

The USA's best bet is to abolish the "Minimum wage law." And pray that unleashing a true genuine free market place won't be too late to allow freedom to survive and not be lost for another ten thousand years.

From a nature point of view, the "Boom and bust cycle is the same as the "Life and death" cycle; at some point its rotation cycle will not be denied. **SIRMANS LOG: 23 SEPTEMBER 2013, 1851 HOURS**

WILL INDIVIDUAL FREEDOM BE WIPED OFF THE FACE OF THE EARTH FOREVER?
I don't think so, but many people do think I preach doom and gloom as a writer. Concerning all of this Obamacare mess, I heard a guy on TV make a profound statement. He said we are not going to be able to unscramble this egg, which I totally agree.

I believe Obamacare is the last straw that is going to break the USA economy's back by exploding the dole.

So, I am hoping when all of the smoke and fog clears A black knight will ride in on a white horse and slay the evil "Minimum wage law" villain, then a true genuine "Free market place" can freely raise up like a Phoenix and save individual freedom from being lost forever. **SIRMANS LOG: 20 SEPTEMBER 2013, 1141 HOURS**

AMERICANS BELIEVE IN SLAVERY AND DON'T REALIZE IT!
This morning I heard a man on TV say he believe that food was a right and also medical care was a right. Now, hardly anyone saw anything wrong with that type of thinking, because practically all liberals and 90 percent of the American population agree with him.

But, I'll tell you with that type of thinking on a wide enough scale there is no way the USA can be saved. Let me interpret what he said. Wisdom wise he and others has no idea what that type of thinking really means or equals to.

Thinking like that equals to saying there is "Something for nothing in life." And believing anyone is entitle to free medical care is the same as believing in slavery. How else is anyone entitle to free medical care unless there are slaves to provide it.

The doctors, nurses, and medical care workers would all have to be slaves for anyone to be entitle to free medical care. That said, I will say again for the umpteenth time, only "Abolishing the minimum wage law" can save this great nation.

Doing that will untie what made this a great exceptional nation in the first place, a true genuine "Free market place."

Oh! OK! Now I see! We are entitle to free food and medical care because the government is our daddy provider and should pay for it, (SMDH) shake my damn head. Sure, that-a-work until there are more free loaders riding in the wagon than pushing the wagon.

After all everyone loves riding a free horse or a grave train. **SIRMANS LOG: 19 SEPTEMBER 2013, 1043 HOURS**

A SWEET LITTLE SUGAR PIE!
Folks, I take no pleasure in taking a stand on something I know 98 percent of the American people disagree with me on. But, I am driven by some unknown force to sound the distress call to survive.

We are human being and we all are controlled by self-interest and emotions. That mean in the grand theme of things it won't really matter what the democrats do, what the republicans do, or what tax changes are made. The USA economy is still going to totally collapse. That is because what got us here in the first place self-interest and emotions haven't changed.

Our survival must be turned over to a system that has never failed, that system will do what must be done to assure our survival, and that system is a true free market place. But, there is only one thing blocking our way to that true free market place. And that one thing is a sweet little sugar pie.

Her name is "Minimum wage law." She has a spell on all of us. Myself, I plead abstinent.
SIRMANS LOG: 13 SEPTEMBER 2013, 2213 HOURS

WORLD POWER CHESS GAME, NEXT MOVE!
Suppose there are world leaders that read my work and don't believe the USA will ever abolish the minimum wage law. That means the USA economy cannot be saved and will soon totally collapse.

You can't stay a great military power without being backed by a great economy, period. Not everyone ignores the great supernatural wisdom of this great writer.

It won't be pretty but abolishing the minimum wage law will allow a true free market place to kick in and save the USA. Trust me; nothing else can save the USA from total doom no matter what the egg heads and learned economist tell you.

A true free market place has never failed in the history of man kind. **SIRMANS LOG: 12 SEPTEMBER 2013, 1039 HOURS**

GUARANTEED WEIGHT CONTROL!
I know that weight control is 90 percent mental. And I do believe in positive thinking to change behavior. So, I repeat to myself over and over at least 50 times or more every day this quote: "I love my slim and healthy body." It has certainly helped me a lot but not overnight it took some time to work.
SIRMANS LOG: 10 SEPTEMBER 2013, 1044 HOURS

RACISM VERSUS SUBJECTIVITY IN AMERICA!
Let's just get real here, reality and subjectivity is two different things. However, some people do have a problem distinguishing between objectivity and subjectivity. We in America are ruled by law not by man or his subjective emotions, thank

God.

We in America probably have more different races and religions than any nation on earth, yet have less friction. The reality is no one race in America is treated extra special, especially the African American race. Now, who and why would anyone advocate that African Americans are treated extra special.

I just don't believe the facts backs up anything of the sort, I suspect there may be a feeling of superiority subjectivity at play here. **SIRMANS LOG: 09 SEPTEMBER 2013, 1545 HOURS**

DYING USA ECONOMY STILL ECONOMIC ENGINE FOR THE WORLD!
Minimum wage, minimum wage, minimum wage equal Ignorance, ignorance ignorance! Almost everyone is focused only on the minimum wage to make more money. But, it is not the minimum wage that is financially killing everyone; it is the buying power and the cost of living that is killing everyone.

It is dumb and one-dimensional economically in a free market place to force any amount of wage or price control on the people. Why do you think most of the world is poor and will always be poor, they won't allow a true free market place?

A forced minimum wage on the people more than anything else has destroyed the USA economy, our nuclear and extended family system, and our moral code. Yet, even a crippled and dying USA economy still has enough free market place capacity left to remain the economic engine of the world.

The Dragons, little Dragons and all other economies of the world would sputter to a screeching halt if the huge USA lifeblood market dried up. So, instead of always focusing only on more money to live on, people need to know the real reason why the cost of everything you buy is too high. Duh.

Water is free; it's the processing and piping you pay for. Whatever happened to being able to live off the land?

Free Market, free market, free market, what a joke. When government forces any wage or price control (minimum wage) on the people there is nothing free about that. Within the next two years we are going to pay an awesome price for this if we survive at all as a nation.

Sure, the intentions on having a minimum wage are good, but the way to hell is paved with good intentions. Economically wise it is insane and we can't and won't survive with a minimum wage in place, period. **SIRMANS LOG: 04 SEPTEMBER 2013, 1053 HOURS**

SLAVE FIELD-HAND MENTALITY GRIP STILL BINDING.
Wake up African American political and spiritual leadership, grow up and take responsibility, you are not a field-hand anymore. You are now up on the hill in the big house now.

You must now take on the responsibility of running the place. You must now create your own jobs and means of making a living. You must set a budget and make sure the family gets fed, whereas as a field-hand all you had to do was work and obey orders.

You are now the master of your own destiny now, if you don't do it yourself it may not get done, you are not a dependent anymore. Fast forward to the year of our Lord 2013, the African American race has a serious problem.

People are afraid of African American men, especially young black males. Reality is reality and it is what it is. There is an old saying: You can't make other people change, but, you can change yourself then the world around you will change.

If you don't believe that here is an example: Stress: If anyone on your job or anywhere causes you a lot of stress, just repeat this quote to yourself over and over as long as necessary, "I can wish all people goodwill no matter how they treat me," then the stress will vanish. This is only a tool and not for every situation.

Black males are stereotyped as dangerous and violent prone. A stereotype can be overcome and gotten rid of. You get rid of a stereotype by proving over time that it is no longer true. But, that can't be done until one accepts responsibility and stop blaming circumstance and the system.

There is no excuse why Africans Americans can't obey the law and behave as good as any race, period. Any winning coach will tell you, you are going to get some bad calls but you focus even harder on your game plan.

Sure, as a minority the system may not give a black man a break and in some cases may even be unfair, still, there is no excuse why African Americans can't obey the law and behave as good as any Race.

I'm over seventy and from the Deep South and I remember before the welfare state destroyed the black family, no one feared a black man walking into a country store.

Many years ago in the USA the Japanese were stereotyped as the junk and trinket merchants. But, through hard work and quality control they proved that they could produce as good a product as any nation. Today no one doubts the quality of Japanese products.

African American political and spiritual leaders need to believe and prove that the African American race can behave and obey the law as good as any race, period. Like me or hate me, still, how can any self-respecting responsible African American disagree with me on this, (SMH) shake my head.

The black community itself suffers more than anyone from all of this violence. Do-for-myself responsible hands need to grab the MLK, Jr. baton and take it into the home stretch to full equality and justice.

And, tell the liberals we don't need your pity or patronizing services any longer **SIRMANS LOG: 27 AUGUSTA 2013, 2135 HOURS**

IS MASS STARVATION AND SUFFERING

AHEAD FOR THE USA?

Almost everyone thinks that I'm really the nut and stupid one for constantly wanting to eliminate the minimum wage law entirely.

Well, I know and anyone with a deep understanding of economics knows that the USA and world economy may soon collapse. When this happens the minimum wage law will disappear and there may be chaos, mass suffering, and starvation if we survive at all.

So, all I'm saying is why go through all of that un-necessarily
when voluntarily abolishing the minimum wage law will prevent it. One way or another the minimum wage will go the way of the great Auk, (SMDH) shake my damn head.

Obamacare is simply the straw that is going to break the camels back.

SIRMANS LOG: 25 AUGUST 2013, 1834 HOURS

"OUR FALSE GOD OF DOOM!"

Just like the big enemy armored divisions of World War II ran on ball bearings our liberal created welfare state runs on the minimum wage law. In sheer economic terms the minimum wage law is "Our false God of doom."

It is impossible to save the USA or western civilization unless the minimum wage law death grip is broken. The laws of economics demands that the minimum wage law must go or the USA bites the dust.
SIRMANS LOG: 24 AUGUST 2013, 0625 HOURS

YOUNG CHILDHOOD SEXUAL ABUSE!
This doesn't belong here and I shouldn't be saying it anyway, it concerns childhood sexual abuse. My view is very simple; if you do the crime you do the time or pay with your life, period.

The good book says flee from temptation, which a wise man will heed to. Contrary to what most people may think there are abnormal forces out there that are almost impossible to resist unless one flees.

Example: A young child sexually abused may become obsessed with sex and become armed with the power of sexual projection. The child grows up but the abnormal power of projection remains. Now, if someone with this abnormal power focuses it on you for whatever reason, your best bet is to get the hell out of Dodge and fast.

Enough said, something like this is never talked about anyway. Ignorance is bliss and just thank God nothing like this has ever happened to you. Believe it or not there are forces out there that only a strong moral and spiritual person can withstand, it's rare, but, it does exist.

"The human mind is a very powerful thing".
SIRMANS LOG: 20 AUGUST 2013, 1138 HOURS

IS A GOVERNMENT SHUTDOWN INEVITABLE?
Right or wrong the republicans are stupid if they force any issue that will end in a government shut down. It will be a lose, lose situation for republicans any way you look at it.

The liberals including the vast majority of the mass media in my view will have a blaming field day. Besides, after the first huge public outcry the vast majority of the republicans will head for the tall grass or high tail it out of Dodge anyway. And even if the republicans could win some kind of hollow victory, very little would change, we still remain a welfare state.

This welfare state is on automatic pilot and nothing or nobody is going to stop it unless its fuel is cut off. Sure, a collapse will stop it but no sane reasonable person wants that, cutting spending won't stop it that will only get the republicans out of office.

Believe it or not, the fuel that propels this whole welfare state is the minimum wage. It is impossible for the USA to survive as a welfare state. But, it is also impossible for the USA to get out of being a welfare state when government sets any wage or price control.

You can't have a true free market economy when government sets any amount of wage or price control. The minimum wage law allows government to inflate the currency so it can keep its power as a super social and family provider.

But, government should never be a social and family provider in the first place because that destroys the nuclear and extended family system. Without a strong nuclear family system it is impossible to remain a free people after four generations.

If the republicans really want to go to the mat for something do something sane like abolishing the minimum wage law entirely. That is the only thing that can save our great nation. yeah! I know! I stand alone on knowing this fact. **SIRMANS LOG: 4 AUGUST 2013, 2210 HOURS**

A Freddie L. Sirmans quote:
Abolishing the minimum wage law will drain the swamp. The swamp is where the welfare state beast lives. The swamp is where all of the anti-survival morality snatchers are coming from. The anti-survival morality snatchers are slowly taking over all of our souls.

TRIVIA NOTE:
Holiday Street in Valdosta, GA. is located within a few yards of where the home was located of the famous western gun fighter "Doc Holiday." It was where he lived as a teenager before going to dental school and heading out west.

WISDOM NOTE:
No one can achieve the great supernatural wisdom that I have without paying an awesome price to survive, and in my case it has been a knockout drag out mentally battle to survive practically all of my life. Still, I have no monopoly on pain or struggle.

PASSING THOUGHT:
If abolishing the minimum wage law is not going to be taken seriously by the USA I'm beginning to suspect the Mayan calendar may not be very far off the mark after all.

FOREWORDS:
Economic ignorance galore abounds, that's

what it is: This caller made a profound statement on TV this morning, his view was that the tax payers were the source of all government funding. Wow! This guy was on to something and he knew more than most, but, he was wrong. Okay, let's do a walk through.

Government funding does come from the tax payers, but, where do the tax payers get their money? All tax payers get their money from their employers or some type of business transaction, period. It goes further; still we haven't arrived at the source of all government funding.

The real source is what gives in my view the shallow minded liberals a problem and is the reason liberals with total power is so dangerous to freedom and democracy. The true answer is: All government funding comes from some type of private business profit.

It is all about profit, profit, and more profit and that can come only from private enterprise. The government can only tax profit or the result of some type of profit, otherwise it cannot survive, period.

In general the shallow minded liberals hate the word profit and too a lesser degree hate business people. The welfare state is the reason the man or woman on the street has no concept of the true role of profit except personally having cash in hand.

You can't get blood out of a turnip and government can't tax where no profit is made. Look at Detroit and California all bastions of liberalism. Unless the minimum wage law is abolished to break the liberal death choke hold on the throat of America that will be the picture of the whole country. God save America!

Liberals are who they are and they love America as much as I do even if I do think they are shallow. It is not entirely the liberals fault, it is the system that got us in our dire situation and only the system can save us, that is why the minimum wage law must be abolished entirely.

Everyone wants to make more money and no one want to make less when we can't make ends meet as it is. But, my great supernatural wisdom know abolishing the minimum wage law is the only way out for the USA to survive, period.

If not for the minimum wage law the cost of living for the poor and everyone would drop so they could pay their own food and doctor bills especially with nuclear family help. But, then the government would lose its God like power as a super provider.

The minimum wage law is blocking everything we buy from dropping down where the poor can pay out of pocket like a free market has always worked before the "New deal." It is the buying power of money that truly matters, not some inflated worthless high number. **SIRMANS LOG: 24 JUNE 2013, 1123 HOURS**

USA CRIMINAL JUSTICE SYSTEM IS NOT PERFECT BUT STILL THE WORLDS BEST. Let me try to shine some light on this. In the USA we have an adversarial criminal justice system which is not perfect but overall still the fairest known to man.

The prosecutor tries everything it can to win the case and on the other hand the Defense tries everything it can to prevent losing the case. Well. Most of the time somewhere in the middle justice will be realized but not always.

The system is not about emotions, right or wrong, or feelings because then justice would always be one-sided and never balanced. However, Joe six-pack and most laymen's believe that if you commit the first wrong and a tragedy result the blame is on you, period.

Sure, Christianity allows mercy and forgiveness, but, when you set a tragedy in motion you can't expect a pat on the back and hero worshiping unless racial bias is involved.

The biggest loser in this whole thing could end up being the Democratic Party. That is because if the blacks stay pissed-off enough they may stay home during the mid term election next year.

This is a dire survival situation in the eyes of most blacks; yet, I for one believe there is some un-necessary stoking of this highly emotional matter. Cooler and calmer heads is what's needed, instead of a lot of flamboyant rhetoric that fans the flames. **SIRMANS LOG: Updated 17 JULY 2013, 1103 HOURS.**

OK:
I have commented on this tragedy, so I might as well go whole hog and say what I really feel about the overall African American situation. But, this is an emotional charged issue and I know that truth and reasoning's won't win me a popularity contest.

Sure, there is racialism in America, always has been and always will be. However, racialism may be an obstacle but that is not what is holding African Americans back or down, especially in this day and time. Before the welfare state came along African Americans faced slavery and a far harsher climate than today, Yet, still owned far more.

I'm going to cut right through the chase and strike right at the heart of the African American community problem. I think as a rule African Americans still has a slavery dependency mentality and don't feel entirely responsible for their own survival as a race.

African Americans are stereotyped as violent prone, criminal prone, likely to lower property values, and bring social baggage in most cases. Whoa, anybody thinking that must be a racialist, maybe or maybe not.

What is never said or admitted is every stereotype has a truth foundation. And you can't dismiss a stereotype by ignoring it and making excuses for bad behavior. When bad behavior is excused and ignored it will reflect on the entire race. And it is not facing reality to think otherwise.

Yet, ignoring that fact is typical liberal behavior. By the African American leadership not taking responsibility for our own behavior as a race causes us all to suffer the consequences of being stereotyped in a bad way. Jealousy, envy, sibling rivalry, and a host of negative emotions come along with having a dependent mentality.

Whereas one with an independent mentality tends to soars above the negative stuff, and will accept total responsibility for himself, his race, and his country. As to jobs, the white man is expected to supply all of the jobs. There are plenty of African Americans with plenty of money, why shouldn't blacks as race be expected to supply more of their own jobs to their community.

I could go on and on but I think I made my point; we need to get a grip and feel totally responsible. I don't have the answer but I do know before the welfare state no one feared black men. Before you can solve a problem you first must admit you have a problem.

I say the African American community has a problem facing up to the truth. And I think it boils down to taking total responsibility for one's own survival. The surest way to cure dependency is to have the props and crutches taken away, but that can't happen as long as we have a welfare state.

Denying truth is the same as denying reality. And that is exactly what African Americans leadership and spiritual leaders have been doing for years concerning black crime. I have no power to stop bad behavior or crime, but, you can bet your bottom dollar that I will never condone it or make excuses for it no matter who does it.

Folks, I have no power to change anything, I'm just thankful I can still write and say what I believe. God Bless America. **SIRMANS LOG: 19 JULY 2013, 2234 HOURS**

USA SUPREME COURT CONFIRMS THE VALIDITY OF MY WRITING! For over twenty years even I at times have questioned the worth or validity of my writing. But, not anymore, since the supreme court all but struck down the defensive marriage act on 26 JUNE 2013.

Folks, it's over for the great USA and western civilization. And the really sad part is very few people even realize it. It is very simple, there has never been and never will be a civilization that last over 80-100 years without a strong nuclear and extended family system, period.

What the Supreme Court did was drive the

final nail in the coffin of a strong nuclear and extended family system. Now! Let me tell you why I know I am right beyond a shadow of a doubt. The nuclear and extended family system has kept civilization intact for over 6,000 years.

That was until the early 1930's in the USA when a group of liberal geniuses did something that had never been done in the history of mankind; they seized the family provider role for the government itself. Wow! Wham! Bam! Armed with the "New deal" programs the government became "The great white father" and sugar daddy.

What the shallow minded liberals failed to realize and still haven't to this day is understand that the provider role is the Key to civilization and its survival. What is taught and instilled in the young is what maintains and keep society stable and intact.

Norms and traditions must be instilled for safety and survival because they are based on past trial and experience. This must duty for over 6,000 years was tasked to the provider of each nuclear family unit. The nuclear family provider is the only one with the power and authority to make sure this must duty is carried out.

The family provider should have the physical, financial, and moral capacity to perform this duty thereby safeguarding and maintaining a healthy civilized society. Well, we all know what happened; the USA government seized the provider role for itself and got drunk on power. So, you can forget about it yielding even one inch, ever.

Sure, it provided food and shelter, but failed to enforce any other must provider duty. Failure by the government as the provider to make sure norms and traditions were instilled in the young meant death to the USA four generations into the future. And sure enough here we are around four generations later with almost everything ass backward.

Same sex marriage and mass killing in the womb seem to be the norm today which would have been insane at the time, and now sound judgment is something you find in the history books. And, you are going to convince me that this nation can survive, @#%$*%$#, I love you too!

But, due to my great supernatural wisdom I see one last chance for the USA to survive. And we can still survive with freedom still intact provided we as a nation abolish the minimum wage law; otherwise we go the way of the great Auk. **SIRMANS LOG: 27 JUNE 2013, 1255 HOURS**

THE FULL DESTRUCTIVE FORCE OF OBAMACARE IS FIXING TO HIT!
All seems to be calm and quiet on the home front; they say the housing market is booming. So, what is there to fear? It is almost always quiet before the storm. I'll tell you what's lurking out there, the full destructive force of Obamacare is about to hit.

I also predict that the dole is likely to explode and then all hell is going to break lose when Obamacare fully hit. So, my advice is brace yourself the s... is about to hit the fan. There is already a mad rush by businesses to stay below 50 employees and keep the work week below 30 hours.

There is already over 48,000.000 million on the food stamps dole alone, plus, we are already $17,000.000.000.000 trillion in debt and borrowing 40 cents of every dollar the government spends. Now, you are going to convince me otherwise that at some point the USA government is not going to prostitute our sovereignty away?#@%!, spare me.

So, in a few more months when Obamacare fully kicks in it may be Katie bar the door. In my view everything Washington enacts now if it's not to abolish the minimum wage law is going to be an exercise in futility.

I think the USA is at a do or die stage, and dealing with the root problem first is a must and anything else is a waste of precious time. I see the USA destructive root problem as government's seized role of being a "Social and family provider."

The USA government as a social and family provider has ran it course which is a role it should never have gotten into in the first place. The "New deal" seized the provider role from the nuclear and extended family system where it had been for over 6,000 years.

Until the USA government gets the hell out of the social and family provider business the USA cannot and will not survive, period. It's just that simple, either the USA government jettisons its social and family provider role or we go the way of the great auk, there is no way to get around that fact.

The only way to save the USA before a total economic collapse results from Obamacare and an exploding dole is to abolish the minimum wage law now. I know in today's climate very few has the wisdom or depth to see how abolishing the minimum wage would save the USA economy.

That is why I really don't see the minimum wage ever being abolishing voluntarily, still, I must never stop pounding for it. Even if no one else do I know only abolishing the minimum wage can safely bleed off the pressure and save the USA economy, because there is no doubt in my mind it is fixing to blow or collapse.

Sure, before the "New deal" there was much suffering especially the elderly. But, the tried and true nuclear and extended family provider system has proven itself for over 6,000 years, it's not perfect, but it works and doesn't destroy morality. Plus, the nuclear and extended family provider system is never a threat to bring down the whole system and send us all back to the Stone Age.

Whereas, the "New deal" has given us this tax hungry welfare state socialist beast. This beast has all but destroyed the nuclear family, family values, and sunk our morals to the point that we have same sex marriage and mass killing of the unborn in the womb. And even worse, very few USA citizens even care or give a damn, to them that's just the new norm.

Yet, someone like me is seen as a nut case

and a throw back that should be ignored or locked away some where. With all of this going on the USA cannot and will not survive unless the minimum wage is abolished to bring back some sanity.

We are just too far gone into this swamp of value rot and moral decay, only a physical barrier like abolishing the minimum wage can save us now. Man is control by logic and self-interest which means the way to hell is paved with good intentions.

"Be still God will fight your battle," but, in this case, abolish the "Minimum wage law, then be still, and the invisible hand which is nature's supreme law of "Natural selection" will save the USA economy and western civilization, too. **SIRMANS LOG: 9 MAY 2013, 1243 HOURS.**

FREDDIE L SIRMANS SR. SHORT BASIC LECTURE ON UNDERSTANDING AN ECONOMY!
Am I dumb, ignorant, or just plain stupid, I'm sure many people think so because I keep harping on abolishing the minimum wage law. What if I am a kook or loon, still, that don't prove me wrong. Sure, when you look at it on an individual or personal basis obviously no one want to make less income.

On the surface a minimum wage seems like a good thing just like most things that have create this welfare state beast we have. In my view even most learned economist doesn't really understand how a free market place economy is supposed to work.

The real truth is it is nature's supreme law of "Natural selection" that really controls everything in nature including the working of an economy. And anyone that doesn't understand nature can never understand an economy.

The first understanding is listening to the words, it says natural selection and free market, force is nowhere to be found. So, that means the first rule to understanding an economy is force will never get you the most production out of an economy.

A minimum wage law is the use of force and it slows production and may even bring growth to a halt. Without a minimum wage law many more businesses could start small and grow into giants.

Many big business men will tell you that if they had to start today they could never have gotten off the ground. All a minimum wage really does in terms of progress is give more power to the government to control private property.

The minimum wage law keeps money inflated for government to have enough to pay one group not to work and tax the other group to death which allows government to stay drunk on power. Right now the government have taken over and own far more private property than a hundred years ago and will probably end up owning it all.

Another reason why people don't understand economics is first you have to understand human nature to understand economics. A good example is "Greed," almost everyone thinks greed is a bad thing for an economy, wrong; nothing could be further from the truth.

Nothing can replace greed. There is no greater energy packed motivating force in our entire human makeup than greed. Greed is something that must be harnessed, but, never smothered out or severely restricted if you want a successful economy.

There has never been a rich and prosperous nation without a lot of greedy people to make it happen. Greed can be compared to electricity, very dangerous, but very little progress can be made in terms of wealth without it.

A free market place with free competition is the perfect way to harness greed without smothering or snuffing it out, like the communist or socialist. There never have been and never will be a rich and prosperous pure communist or socialist state.

The USA is no longer even close to having a genuine free market place. A genuine free market economic have never in history failed to produce far more than that nation can use in almost everything.

Yet those in power that love power and control may tolerate the free market but still hate it. The reason power hungry leaders don't like the free market is kin or no kin if you don't produce you are gone.

In closing I will add this little nugget: To create great wealth one must be willing to take great risk. But, no one is going to take great risk without a fair chance for a great reward, period. Why work extra hard and produce more when non producers get an equal share that is where the great USA seems to be headed.

I hope my short economic lecture have been helpful to you in some way. I am a creative self-made writer; most of what you get is my own original thinking.

SIRMANS LOG: 16 MAY 2013, 2056 HOURS.

EXTRA INPUT: 23 MAY 2013, 0135

HOURS.

Let me say this to around 95 percent of the USA population that strongly disagrees with me and my views on abolishing the minimum wage law, there is a very important question that you have failed to ask.

That question is: what are you and the country going to do when the USA government doesn't have the money and can't borrow it to pay its bills. Huh! That's the problem! Over 95 percent of the USA population have never imagined let alone asked a question of the sort.

Almost everyone seems to think of the USA government as some kind of omnipotent money sow that we can suck on her tits forever. But, nothing could be further from the truth. There never has been and never will be a government that doesn't go broke at some point.

Even worse, the USA has a social and family provider government that amounts to a socialist welfare state. The USA economy not only can collapse it will collapse as soon as Obamacare fully kicks in in a few months.

No matter what the learned economist and egg heads may tell you, self-made writer little ole me is telling you the USA economy is on the brink and when Obamacare fully kicks in it will collapse.

Sure, probably no one is going to believe me, no problem, we all will know in a few months if the USA economy can swallow Obamacare and survive.

Of course, any suspense could be avoided if the USA just took the bull by the horns and abolished the minimum wage law which would no doubt save the USA economy.

THE "NEW DEAL" CURSE!
Family discipline is the extremely important ingredient that has been missing in the USA ever since the "New deal" seized the provider role from the nuclear and extended family system.

The nuclear and extended family system is where the provider role stayed for over 6,000 years until the "New deal" seized it in the name of Mr. Do-gooder.

However, being a provider is much, much more than just providing food and shelter. The provider is the only one with the power and control to enforce and maintain discipline and instill it in the young.

For any society to survive over four generations the provider must safeguard norms and traditions and make sure they are instilled in the young.

So, when the shallow minded liberals armed with the "New deal" seized the provider role for itself it failed to take on provider duties and responsibilities that have been carried out for over 6,000 years. And the liberals are still doing this crime against USA society.

This shallow senseless liberal destruction has devastated and all but destroyed the African American community in the USA and the cancer is well on it's way to destroying all of USA society.

Now, here we are in the year of our Lord two thousand thirteenth year with 95 percent of the USA population left with the survival instinct of a 10 year old.

We are at death door in terms of human survival with all of our eggs in one basket. We solely depend on a bloated wobbly kneed socialist welfare state beast that could totally collapse any moment and send civilization all the way back to the stone age.

No society can survive without a strong nuclear and extended family system, a strong moral and spiritual code in place, and adequate emergency backup bartering capacity with many small farmers and home gardeners.

Those were the survival tools that allowed western civilization to survive the great depression, which today is practically nonexistent. The stone age may be our only destination.

That is because nature's law of "Boom and Bust" is like the life and death cycle there can be no long term survival unless it is carried out. Yet, here I am with an almost super natural strong survival instinct and I'm seen as a nut, kook, loon, or some other reject or hater.

I plead and I plead for sanity like abolishing the minimum wage law which I know will save my beloved homeland, the only home I know.

Having this great wisdom and super strong survival instinct is like a curse to me; I can dissect an economy and see straight to the core of most things when so many just don't get it. God, I ask in your name bless the USA home of the brave and the free.

MAN HAS NEVER SET FOOT ON THE MOON? SIRMANS LOG: 02 JUNE 2013,

1750 HOURS Awhile back I wrote an article that I was 99.9 percent sure that man landed on the moon but I still can't get past that .1 percent. It's not that I am dumb or stupid; I understand electronics and modern science.

Right out of high school back in 1962 I took a six month course in radio and TV repair. Back then we studied mainly the super heterodyne receiver and vacuum tubes. The transistor was just coming into play the same as the cathode ray vacuum tube which was the early TV.

We also learned about waves and frequencies. So, on my part it just doesn't make any sense for me to doubt that they landed on the moon. When I wrote the first article on this subject a guy asked me in a comment did I have any proof that they didn't land on the moon, and I said "No."

In replying I told him it was just a gut feeling, and that is still what haunts me on how I feel about the whole matter. There is something about this whole thing that logical just doesn't add up in my way of thinking. I feel something is wrong somewhere.

Even if they did land, maybe they found something up there (UFO) that they are not telling. I have a fair understanding of human nature, and there have never been a case where man opened up a new frontier and didn't exploit it in some way.

Like I said, maybe there is a big hidden mystery that maybe it's better the public never knows about. I don't have any inside information, just a raw gut feeling. This article may be the smoking gun or the last straw that I really am a nut, kook, or loon, who cares, some already believe that anyway.

However, I am not entirely alone doubting that man landed on the moon, 10 percent of the USA population is Doubting Thomas's on this. God bless America.

THE USA LAST SUPPER! SIRMANS LOG: 9 JUNE 2013, 1954 HOURS. Anyone that can stomach reading my work knows that I have a super mind agree or not. So, I have decided to draw a picture and explain what happened to the great USA. I think it boils down to two word "Sound judgment."

Starting with me, probably three percent or less of the USA population agree or truly understand my way of thinking. The vast majority think my writing is some kind of nineteenth century throwback. And they are mostly right, a hundred years ago about ninety five percent of the USA population would have agreed with my way of thinking.

Back then same sex marriage and mass killing in the womb would have been beyond everyone's imagination. Now, ninety five percent or more of the USA population see that as normal. The USA is about evenly split down the middle in terms of voting.

The masses of government dependents see the republicans as the enemy and believe they would like to take away their livelihood. The other half believes the democrats are going to tax and spend the USA out of existence. But, I believe like one politician said: "There is not a dime worth of difference between the two parties."

Sure, there are minor differences in terms of appointing judges but neither party is going to serious stop the growth of government. Overall the Dems and liberals are the reason the USA is in the dire situation it is today. In my view Dems and liberals are just plain shallow, but, super aggressive and will not let morality, country, or anything stand in the way of them grabbing and taking power.

On the other hand the Republican Party has become almost as liberal as the democrat party. I feel the conservatives ought to just flat out take it over. Even conservatives don't agree with my out dated thinking, still I think they are the only ones that can save the USA from total doom.

The thing is they don't know how. Well, it may already be too late but I am going to tell them how to save the USA. However, I'm sure they won't agree and won't take my advice; still I'm going to pass it on anyway. Remember, I said the Key words were "Sound judgment." The Dems and liberals own the thinking and shaping of young minds in the USA.

For over 6,000 years up until the "New deal" the nuclear and extended family system was the primary shaper of young minds, but, not anymore. To a great extent in most situations now the primary shaper of young minds is liberal TV and the liberal school systems. Very few homes are instilling traditional conservative's norms and values.

Almost everything the young comes in contact with now-a-days is liberal. So, of course the young when they mature will not have a conservative foundation to return to like children of old. "Sound judgment" which is everything to keep and maintain a civil society will soon be nowhere to be found.

So, my advice to conservatives is follow my advice cold turkey and go for the jugular. No if ands or buts, fight to abolish the minimum wage law now, not tomorrow. With no minimum wage law the government will lose it power to control private property.

With no minimum wage law government would have to give up its provider role which has all but destroyed our nuclear and extended family system. With no minimum wage law manufacturing would return to the USA and everything would be made in America with jobs for all.

With no minimum wage law the economy would balance itself and the poor could pay their own food and medical bills. With no minimum wage law people would make far less money but $5.00 would buy A week's worth of grocery. And I could go on and on what has been proven to work for over 6,000 years before the "New deal."

Plus here are the cold steel facts, if the minimum wage law is not abolished, the USA is not going to survive and that is a guarantee. Before the "New deal" the male nuclear family provider hands on instilled and enforced norms and traditional conservatives values thereby safe guarding our human survival.

Now, unless the government is kicked out of the provider role the USA has the chance of a snowball in hell of surviving. Abolishing the minimum wage will get the ball rolling on saving my beloved homeland.

I believe in a few months when Obamacare fully kicks in it is going to explode the dole and cause the USA economy to crash and burn. I also believe abolishing the minimum wage law is the only way to stop the USA economy from crashing and burning.

Will congress abolish the minimum wage law? NO! Will the USA and western civilization survive? NO! Reason, the boom and bust cycle is a part of nature the same as the life and death cycle.

Abolishing the minimum wage law would have save us by allowing the bust cycle to complete it normal rotation, but no, the learned economist and egg heads think they can juggle the figures forever, wrong.

Call me a fool or nut as you wish, but without a doubt I know I am right on this. Sure, no one agrees with me on any of this but they will, the hardship and suffering just hasn't taken it toll yet.

ENJOY THIS GREAT LITTLE FABLE BY ME, FREDDIE L SIRMANS SR.

Chapter 1
  Once upon a time there was a little town called Health-land kingdom, located right off the big super MD highway leading to the great cure-all metropolis. In this town lived vitamins, minerals, herbs, humans, and other nutrients.

The town's main goal was to keep all of its citizens healthy because anyone that they failed to keep healthy would have to face terrible traffic jams on the super MD highway leading to the great cure-all metropolis.

  Jim-Niacin (vitamin B-3). Jim-Niacin doesn't stand alone; he is a member of the very powerful B vitamin family. In Health-land Jim-Niacin's job is essential to promote life and good health. He regulates the metabolism and assists in other body processes, even though he is needed in small amounts compared to proteins and carbohydrates.

As a coenzyme Jim-Niacin works
to make sure the human body
functions as it should. There are two
major types of vitamins: the water
soluble and the oil soluble. Jim-Niacin
belongs to the water-soluble type vitamins,
therefore his doses
must be replaced everyday because
the human body doesn't store his
doses like the oil soluble type.

Since Jim-Niacin is only one
member of the very powerful B
vitamin family he shouldn't work
alone; he should be balanced with
other B vitamin members. Jim-Niacin
is not a bad or evil fellow, but he does
have a bad reputation.

Humans are afraid of Jim-Niacin
and rightly so because in too high
doses he may damage the liver, or in
too low doses he does no good. But,
that is not the only reason human
fear Jim-Niacin. Jim-Niacin deals with
circulation and the skin, and he will
heat the skin up like it is on fire and
turn it as red as a beet.
When this happens to a human
for the first time, it will scare some
humans half to death, but don't be put
off, the flushing of the skin is normal
when dealing with Jim-Niacin. It's not
pretty or pleasant but that is how Jim-

Niacin unclogs the capillaries and small blood vessels throughout the body.

      Captain Fredrico (human). Orry Fredrico is one of many humans that Was born and raised in Health-land Kingdom. Orry Fredrico is a Carpenter by trade, but as long as he Could remember he loved the sea. As a small child he would stand by The ocean for hours just staring out to Sea.
      As a teenager he would try to Hop aboard any boat going salt water Fishing. During his senior year in high School he went on one of those deep Sea fishing cruises that goes out for Four or five hours at a time. On this Cruises he met Jan Flemmings. Jan Also loved the sea and they instantly Became attracted to each other. Within days Jim started dating Jan.

      VC (vitamin C). VC also belongs To the water-soluble type of vitamin. VC is truly a heavyweight among Vitamins. VC is known as a very Power antioxidant. He is a mighty Human body protector. He protects the human body against harmful effects of pollution. He helps to prevent cancer. He helps to lower cholesterol and other protection functions.

Scurvy is a disease that moves in when there is a deficiency in vitamin C protection. Years ago, passengers on ships on long voyages without fresh fruits and vegetables had a problem dealing with scurvy.

Jan Flemmings (human). Jan is a Health-land Kingdom toy soldier's brat. Just like Captain Fredrico she has always loved the sea. She was mostly unanchored until she met her soul mate Orry Fredrico. At first she thought he loved the sea too much and would not be a good provider, but his dreamy bedroom eyes soon won her over.

VE (vitamin E). VE belongs to the oil soluble type of vitamin. VE is another mighty antioxidant. VE is very important in fighting cancer and cardiovascular disease. Vitamin E is a giant in so many ways. VE is a natural blood thinner. He promotes good blood circulation, he promotes healthy skin, healthy hair, and so many other healthy body functions. Vitamin E actually belongs to a family of eight but falls into two major groups. These two groups are tocopherols and tocotrienols. It is the alpha-tocopherols form that is the most potent. That is the group VE belongs to.

John-Pyridoxine (vitamin B-6). John-Pyridoxine like his cousin Jim-Niacin is a member of the very powerful B vitamin family. The fact is John-Pyridoxine is involved in more bodily functions than any other single nutrient. John-Pyridoxine deals with both the mental and physical health.

He deals with water retention, sodium and potassium balance, and fights hard against allergies, arthritis, asthma, carpal tunnel syndrome, and on and on. Just like his cousin Jim-Niacin, John-Pyridoxine shouldn't fight alone; he should be balanced with other members of the mighty B vitamin family.

Mister Disease. Mister and his family   showed up one day in Health-land Kingdom. No one seems to know where he came from. All anyone knows is he is mean and evil. He has no friends and is known to attack humans sometimes without provocation.

He has no conscience and will attack anyone that is weak and helpless. The town and kingdom has tried to keep him out, but somehow he always sneaks back in. Our vitamins, minerals, herbs and others nutrient citizens have done a good job fighting him off, but Mister Disease is a very, very tough customer.

Jim-Niacin and the other nutrient protectors of Health-land Kingdom were joyfully patting themselves on the back because they were doing a good job protecting the city's population from Mister Disease and his cohorts. Jim-Niacin decided to telephone his cousin John-Pyridoxine. Jim could hear the phone making its fourth ring.

"Hello," said John-Pyridoxine.
" This is Jim-Niacin, I decided to give you a call and touch base on a matter that I've been tossing around in my mind lately."
"Tell me about it," said John-Pyridoxine.

"Well, I've been thinking that all of the vitamins, minerals, humans, herbs, and other nutrient citizens should get together and have a big town hall meeting. What do you think."

"I think it is a very good idea," said john-Pyridoxine.
" Good, then it's a go, I'm going to start right away making plans," said Jim-Niacin. "John you take care now, I'll talk to you later."
" Bye," said John-Pyridoxine.

Chapter 2

     Orry Fredrico and Jan Flemmings got married after a one year engagement. Orry got an associate degree in carpentry from the local technical college. Twenty five years later Orry and Jan are now the parents of a seventeen-year-old son Rob, and a fifteen-year-old daughter Melinda.

Almost everyone calls Orry by his nickname Captain Fredrico after he bought his first boat about fifteen years ago. The boat was a fourteen footer with a big Mercury motor. Captain Fredrico now operates his own contracting business.

It is almost six o'clock p.m. when Captain Fredrico lets himself in the carport door which opens directly into the kitchen. He found his wife Jan bending over checking her meat loaf in the oven.

"Hello dear," said Captain Fredrico in a somewhat tired voice.
" Hello Orry, how did your day
" Pretty good, but my right wrist that's been bothering me the last couple of weeks seems to be getting worse, especially at night after I fall asleep. Sometimes I wake up with a numb tingling in my right hand. It feels like somebody is sticking pins in my hands."

"Orry, I think you need to check with one of the vitamin citizens. That sounds like something John-pyridoxine might be able to help you with."

"I think you are right dear, I will give him a call in a few days.

After Marrying Orry, Jan Fredrico decided to postpone a career of her own. Becoming a full time housewife and mother was very fulfilling to Jan. She even took on the awesome job of home schooling her kids.

VC (vitamin c) enjoys his job in Health-land Kingdom taking care of its citizens. He has a very good reputation. Humans were using him probably more than any other vitamin. Being one of the most powerful antioxidants, he was in great demand these days.

In fact, he was being used to fortify many of today's foods. He thought the town hall meeting was a great idea. Why didn't he think of it? The vitamins and other nutrients were doing a good job fighting off Mister Disease, but he knew that they couldn't let their guards down, ever.

Just like VC, VE (vitamin E) is another very powerful antioxidant but of the oil soluble type. VE is probably in even greater demand these days than VC. With so many humans becoming diabetics these days, VE with his natural blood thinning power is a real workhorse. VE is also looking forward to the big town hall meeting coming up soon.

On this Monday morning John-Pyridoxine was kicking back at his office when the phone ring.
" Hello," said John-Pyridoxine.
" May I speak to John-Pyridoxine?" said the voice on the line.

"This is he," said John-Pyridoxine.
" I'm Captain Fredrico and I've been told you may be able to help me concerning an ailment. I believe I have a case of carpal tunnel syndrome."

"You have the right vitamin, that is one of my many areas of expertise."
" Then you will be able to help

me," said Captain Fredrico.

"Hold on a minute, I didn't say that. Let me explain the situation here, then I can tell you what I may be able to do. Listen Captain, I'm going to explain what I do, and it should take care of your problem, but then it may not. If I can't cure it, then I recommend you take the super MD highway to the cure all metropolis."

"I understand," said Captain Fredrico.
" Now, first off," said John-Pyridoxine, "my maximum dose is 300 mg. per day, that way I will not damage any nerves. In most cases 100 mg. of my dose will cure the problem. The golden rule with taking any nutrients is don't take more than the recommended dose, because too much of anything may cause damage, and never take nutrients on an empty stomach. So, Captain if you understood everything I said, come by as soon as possible. We have a walk in policy."

"Thank you sir, I should be there within the hour."

Mister Disease is very upset with himself for being unable to do more damage in Health-land Kingdom. He feels he should be able to bring in more of his friends like cancer, AIDS, and even some of his very old friends like the black plague.

He was getting fed up with those damn vitamins, minerals, herbs, and other nutrients. The thing about those nutrients is they are keeping him from getting a foothold in Health-land Kingdom. He feels that if he could just get a foothold he would be able to start an epidemic.

Mister Disease decided that he would just have to work harder. Sooner or later those humans are going to think that they are safe and slack up on utilizing the nutrients. That is the time he plans to throw his best punch. He feels that if his friend AIDS just keeps up the pressure, he has the best shot at causing an epidemic.

Most humans don't know Jim-Niacin and many of those that do tend to fear and avoid him. As one of the smallest members of the powerful B vitamin family, being unknown is about to change. The reason is Jim-Niacin along with his cousin John-Pyridoxine are the ones that called for and organized the town hall meeting coming up in a few weeks. The whole thing was originally Jim-Niacin's idea.

Since then Jim has invited the town fathers and secured all of the permits needed to stage such an event. Jim has contacted other town nutrients and humans, many of them had never heard of him, or knew who he was.

Chapter 3

Captain Fredrico had lived in Health-land Kingdom all of his life and he loved this town. Captain Fredrico got an invitation from Jim-Niacin to attend the town hall meeting coming up in a few weeks.

Captain Fredrico had heard the name Jim-Niacin before and even knew he was a member of the mighty B vitamin family, but that was about all he knew about Jim-Niacin. He didn't know what kind of work or anything else Jim-Niacin did.

Captain Fredrico had heard that the vitamins and other nutrients citizens had become concerned about the health of Health-land Kingdom. The main work our nutrient citizens do is protect our human population from characters like Mister Disease and his friends.

The nutrients knew that cancer and AIDS had almost destroyed a few other towns in the Kingdom. The town hall meeting got Captain Fredrico to thinking. The mayoral election will be coming up in about a year. Captain Fredrico decided that he was going to throw his hat in the ring. Of course he would have to talk it over with his wife Jan first.

After putting in a hard day's work, on his drive home Captain Fredrico thought about the pesky dry skin that had been plaguing him for years. It has slowly become more and more of a problem as time past.

Now it has become a real nuisance. It has come to the point that he has to lotion down almost his whole body every time he takes a shower.

He feels that is unmanly, only women like to lotion their bodies. He has tried everything, but to no avail.

He had even got on the crowded super MD highway and went to the cure all metropolis, but still to no avail. At the cure all metropolis all they did was to prescribe an extremely expensive body cream that did little better than over the counter creams.

He felt truly at his wits end.
There didn't seem to be any hope, he would just have to accept his miserable fate. As Captain Fredrico let himself in the carport door, Jan was making a salad.
" Hello, dear," said the Captain in a husky sexy voice.

"Hello, sweetheart," said Jan in a wooing voice as she dropped everything and rushed over and planted a seductive kiss on her husband's left cheek.

"Now, you go ahead and clean up, dinner will be ready in a few minutes. By the way Rob complained about a bout of indigestion after lunch."

"Did you check with Mr. Blue Page?" said the Captain.
" Yes, he gave me the names of several nutrients that work in that area. The two nutrients that I decided to use were Stewart-Ginger Root and Henry-Acidolphilus. Each one of them gave me heavy doses to give Rob as needed."

"Good, now let me go ahead and wash up, then you can tell me all about it later." After the Captain and all of the family had sat down to dinner and the blessing was said, the Captain revisited the subject of Rob's indigestion.

"How is your stomach feeling now, Rob," said the Captain.
" It's fine now, dad, since Mom had a couple of the nutrients treat it."
" I wasn't sure what to do until after my talk with Mr. Blue Page," said Jan.

"Mr. Blue Page gave me the names of several nutrients that work in the area of indigestion. These are the names that Mr. Blue Page gave me that deal with indigestion: Stewart-Ginger Root, Calvin-Fenugreek, Bonnie-Papaya, Henry-Acidophilus, and Sammy-Oat bran tablets.

He also stressed that they did their work with either tablets or capsules."

"Excuse me for changing the subject, I have a very important announcement to make," said the captain.

"Jan, the mayoral election is coming up in about a year and I would like to know if you have any objections to me throwing my hat into the ring."

"Gee, I don't know? I've never thought about being a politician's wife. Do you think you can win?"
"Dad, I love it, I think it is a great idea," said Melinda.
"Me too," said Rob.

"I can't guarantee you I will win, but I believe if I get out there and shake enough hands I'll have a very good shot."
" Dad, I'll campaign for you," said Melinda.

"Honey, If you really want to run, then count me in as your number one supporter," said Jan.

"Then it's all settled You are looking at the next mayor of Health-land Kingdom."

Ever since John-Pyridoxine had agreed to help his cousin Jim-Niacin organize the big town hall meeting coming up soon, he had stayed busy calling and talking to the citizens of Health-land Kingdom.

Chapter 4

Mr. Disease was aware of the big town hall meeting coming up in a few days, and he definitely was not pleased about what he was hearing. The word was they were going to try to get rid of him. Mr. Disease was not going to let that deter him, that had been tried before with his ancestors all throughout history.

Sure, the discovery of DDT, penicillin, and modern antibiotics had given his family some big setbacks, but some of his old friends like tuberculosis were beginning to make a comeback, and the new kid on the block, AIDS, was really beginning to raise hell.

Mr. Disease felt that as far as he

was concerned, let them have all of the town hall meetings they want to, it was not going to put him out of business.

Mr. Disease watches the super MD highway often and as far as he could tell it was becoming even more crowded each day. Even at the big super cure all metropolis they haven't been able to get rid of his best friend Mr. Cancer. Mr. Cancer is still doing an awful lot of damage.

On this Monday morning Jan Fredrico sure didn't want to battle the traffic jams on the super MD highway going to the cure all metropolis. It was just one of those days, Her daughter was down with a cold and she herself was dealing with a slight kidney infection.

She didn't know? Maybe it was something she ate that was causing her back a slight ache in the area of her kidney. She knew that it would save her a lot of money and time if she called Mr. Blue Page and found out which vitamins, minerals, herbs, or other nutrients that specialized in the areas of their ailments.

Jan decided to give the nutrients twenty-four hours to do their work, then if there was no obvious improvement she would get on the crowded super MD highway to the cure all metropolis. Jan dialed Mr. Blue Page. The voice on the line said, " You have reached Mr. Blue Page directory."
"Mr. Blue Page, this is Jan Fredrico. My daughter has a cold and my kidneys have a slight ache. I would like for you to give me the names of the nutrients that specialize in the areas of our illness."

"Very well, madam. In the area of the kidneys, the association of VC and Cranberry handle that, and in the area of colds and flu, the association of Garlic, Echinacea, and Golden Seal handle that. Will that be all, madam?"

"Yes sir, and thank you very much," said Jan. Taking advantage of their-walk in policy, Jan didn't have to wait long before she was able to see VC, the very powerful vitamin C antioxidant.

"Mrs. Fredrico," said VC, " We give our doses in mostly tablet form.

I am of the water soluble type, the body does not store my doses. Taking too much of my dose is washed out with the urine. But, taking too much of my dose also may cause diarrhea or stomach soreness in some humans.

Rule number one for dealing with your kidney problem is to keep drinking lots of water, then take 2000 mg. of vitamin C tablets three or four times a day after a meal, also take 2000 mg. of cranberry fruit capsules three of four times a day after a meal. That should take care of your problem, Mrs. Fredrico."

Jan next proceeded to take her daughter by the association of Garlic, Echinacea, and Golden Seal to take care of her cold. After a short wait Jan and her daughter were lead in to see Hannah-Garlic.

Hannah-Garlic came from one of the most powerful and popular of all herb families. Even the Roman army would not go into battle without a member of the garlic family coming along.

Hannah-Garlic instructed Jan to give Melinda throat lozenges if needed, then give her a dose of about 1400 mg. of odor controlled garlic, three or four times a day after a meal, also give her a 1500 mg. dose of combination echinacea-golden seal three or four times a day after a meal.

"You should see some obvious improvement in twenty four hours; if not take the super MD highway to the cure all metropolis.

"It is also helpful to take heavy doses of vitamin C after a meal at the beginning of a cold. But, only at the beginning of a cold, because if congestion sets in, vitamin C tends to make it worse. Warning: Never take vitamin C or others nutrients on an empty stomach," she said.
After thoroughly going over everything, Hannah-Garlic said, " That is it, Mrs. Fredrico, do you understand all of my instructions?"

"Yes, Herb Garlic and thank you very much." While driving home Jan reminded herself to do her neck exercises when she got home. It has been quite awhile since stress has caused her neck to tense up, but she Decided that she would go ahead and do the exercises anyway.

Jan believed that feeling stress is a normal part of life. The better one learns how to deal with life's frustrations the better one will be able to cope with stress. Stress affects people in many different ways. It may affect some in physical ways such as headaches, neck aches, shoulder aches, etc.

To deal with physical aches it is helpful to do these exercises. These exercises are done sitting on the side of the bed. Sit on the side of the bed with feet apart flat on the floor for balance. With both hands rolled into a fist, place them thumbs inward down on the bed several inches from the body on each side.

Start the first exercise by twisting the neck and entire upper body counter-clockwise as far as possible, then twist the neck and entire upper body clockwise as far as possible. Do these exercises in sets of one hundred as many times as one desires.

Start the second exercise by leaning the head as far as possible on the right shoulder, then lean the head as far as possible on the left shoulder. Do these exercises in sets of one hundred as many times as one desires.

Start the third exercise by leaning the chin as far as possible down on the chest, then lift the head backward as far as possible. Do these exercises in sets of one hundred as many times as one desires.

Chapter 5

On the morning of the big town hall meeting, Jim-Niacin followed his daily routine of taking care of the citizens of Health-land Kingdom. Jim-Niacin tried to take care of all loose ends concerning the town hall meeting by making a lot of last minute phone calls. He rehearsed the program with his cousin B-12 who would be the moderator for tonight's town hall meeting.

At seven o'clock p.m. sharp Jim-Niacin arrived at the local high school gymnasium, the location of tonight's town hall meeting. The meeting was scheduled to start at eight o'clock p.m. There were several satellite trucks already in place when he arrived. There were the local radio and TV crews as well as reporters from the big super cure all metropolis.

Arriving at the high school was familiar territory for Captain Fredrico. He had walked at the high school track three or more times a week for several years. The high school track was a popular walking place for the citizens of Health-land Kingdom. Captain Fredrico felt that walking or some type of physical fitness program is a must to maintain good health.

It is a fact that one in good physical condition has almost a ten times better chance of surviving a heart attack, stroke, or any ailment. Also, physical activity plays a big role in controlling diabetes. A big help with diabetes is controlling what one eats. Most humans can control diabetes by cutting way back on starches and sweets and taking a chromium picolinate at each meal.

One needs to eat less meat and include more peas, beans, fresh fruits, and raw vegetables. One needs to include at least one raw fruit or vegetable at each meal because cooking and microwaving food destroys all enzymes and most vitamins.

Enzymes are involved in almost every bodily function, especially the digestive process. Enzymes are mostly divided into two groups: digestive enzymes and metabolic enzymes. The digestive enzymes break down food enabling the body to function properly.

The human body manufactures a limited supply of enzymes, but in order to prevent indigestion and other digestive problems one should get as many enzymes as possible from raw food. Otherwise, the body's limited supply becomes depleted.

Jim could see that there was going to be a very big turnout for tonight's event. It seemed like his hard work on getting the word out had paid off. Several tables were set up at one end of the gymnasium to try to accommodate as many as possible on the big panel of vitamins, minerals, humans, herbs, and other nutrients.

Everyone were handed a program as they filed into the gymnasium. It read that, "We will not be able to accommodate everyone due to the time it would take. The moderator will ask all questions, but he will take a few written questions from the audience." At exactly eight p.m. sharp B-12 (vitamin B-12) strode up to the podium.

"Greetings, my fellow vitamins, minerals, humans, herbs, and other nutrients, I'm B-12 your moderator for tonight's town hall meeting," he said. "First I would like to welcome our town's fathers, celebrities, and all other dignitaries to this town hall meeting. Now, I would like to thank the vitamin that made it all happen. He is truly another unsung hero. Many of you here tonight probably have never heard of him, but all of the while he has been out there everyday doing his job. He is one of the lesser known members of the powerful B vitamin family. I am proud to say this truly unsung hero is my first cousin Jim-Niacin (vitamin B-3). Stand up, Jim."

"Thank you, thank you, thank you," said Jim-Niacin as he stood and the audience loudly applauded. "Now," said B-12, "before we get into questions and answers we are going to let several members on our panel down here give their name and vocation. We will start with me. I'm B-12 (vitamin B-12). One of my many jobs is to assure proper digestion and the absorption of food."

"I'm Jane-Ginkgo Biloba. I'm a very well known herb. I'm mostly Known for improving memory."
"I'm Sammy-Oat Bran Tablets. I'm known for my fiber. Fiber does so many things, for now I will mention just two, I lower the blood cholesterol and help stabilize blood sugar."

"I'm Eddie-calcium. I'm a mineral and I do many things. I'm most needed for strong bones and teeth and to help lower blood pressure."
"I'm Mary-Magnesium. I'm a mineral and of the many things that I do, enzyme activity is most vital. I also assist calcium and potassium uptake."

"I'm Sue-Chromium. I'm a mineral and of the many things that I do, maintaining stable blood sugar levels is most vital."
"I'm VA (vitamin A). I'm a vitamin and lesser known antioxidant. My main job is protecting the eyes and some skin problems."
"I'm Dee Dee (vitamin D). I'm a vitamin, and I'm needed for the absorption of calcium and phosphorus."

"I'm Ned-Zinc. I'm a mineral and of the many things that I do, keeping the prostate gland healthy is most vital."

"I'm Kenny-Saw Pametto. I'm an herb, my main job is to prevent the enlargement of the prostate gland."

"I'm Gina-Evening Primrose Oil. I'm an essential fatty acid. I'm a necessity that cannot be made by the human body. I do many things, but improving the skin is my favorite."

"I'm Patty-Potassium. I'm a mineral. Of my many jobs I will name just a few. I help maintain a healthy nervous system and regulate heart rhythm, also I help control the body's water balance."

"I'm Hannah-Garlic. I'm an herb. I detoxify and protect the body against infections. I help lower blood pressure, aid circulation and perform many other functions."

"I'm Henry-Acidophilus. I'm a friendly bacteria. My main job is to aid digestion."

"I'm Bonnie-Papaya. I'm an herb. I aid digestion. I'm good for heartburn, indigestion, and bowel disorders."

"I'm Brad-Cranberry Fruit. I'm an herb. I'm helpful for fighting infections of the urinary track."

"I'm Stewart-Ginger Root. I'm an herb. I do many things, but cleaning the colon, reducing spasms, and stomach cramps is my favorite."

"I'm Calvin-Fenugreek. I'm good for the stomach, intestines, eyes, asthma, sinus, inflammation, and lung disorders. I also increase sexual desire."

"I'm Edna-Echinacea. I'm an herb. I have anti viral properties and I help boost the immune system. I'm very helpful against colds and flu."
"I'm Gene-Golden Seal. I'm an herb. I act as an antibiotic, and have anti-inflammatory and antibacterial properties."

I'm David-Dandelion root. I am an herb. I help cleanse the blood stream and liver and increase the production of bile. I'm used as a diuretic. I help reduce uric acid and improve functioning of the stomach and other vital organs.

"That is the last introduction we will have time for," said B-12. "Now, I will ask the panel a few written questions given to me from the audience, but first let me explain our role here. Number one is we try to be the first line of defense on protecting Health-land Kingdom from Mr. Disease and his cohorts.

"We have some citizens who don't believe in us and won't use our services. The next thing is we don't try to be everything to everybody, our services and abilities are limited.

We encourage anyone that has doubts or don't believe in us to take the super MD highway to the cure all metropolis. Still, there is a lot we can do to keep Mr. Disease and his friends from gaining a foothold here in Health-land Kingdom.

"Very important: When taking the super MD highway to the cure all metropolis, make sure you tell them which of our services you are maintaining.

"Now, when I ask a question to the panel, please let those that specialize in that particular area of

expertise answer the question. Time will not allow me to ask but only a few questions. My first question to the panel is what can we do to combat prostate disease?" he asked.
"I'm Ned-Zinc, and I recommend 50 mg. of zinc per day."

"I'm Larry-Pumpkin Seed Oil, and I recommend 1000 mg. of pumpkin seed oil per day."
"I'm Kenny-Saw Pametto, and I recommend 160 mg. of saw pametto extract twice per day."
"I'm VE (vitamin E), and I recommend 1000 I.U. of vitamin E per day."
"I'm Jim-Niacin, and I recommend my maintenance dose of 250 mg. of niacin per day."
"Is there anyone else?" said B-12. "So, that gives us five weapons to fight prostate disease, and I'm pretty darn sure that anyone that arms themselves with these weapons will be able to keep Mr. prostate disease away for a very long time, if not forever. My next question to the panel is what can we do to deal with diabetes disease?"

"I'm Sue-Chromium, and I recommend 200 mg. of chromium picolinate three times a day at meal time. I also would like to elaborate a little on this terrible disease.

"Diet plays a major role in controlling this terrible disease. Everyone with this disease should be able to home check his blood sugar level and keep it under control. But, controlling blood sugar is not the only problem diabetics face.

"There are problems with the eyes, blood circulation, and many others. There is a problem with nerve damage (neuropathy) especially in the lower extremities," she concluded.

"I'm VE (vitamin E), and I recommend 1000 I.U. of vitamin E per day. Being a natural blood thinner makes me a great asset to a diabetic."

"I'm Jim-Niacin, and I recommend my maintenance dose of 250 mg. of niacin once per day for one not showing any diabetic symptoms. On the other hand, for anyone experiencing the symptoms of diabetes, especially numbness in the lower extremities I recommend my unclogging dose of 250 mg. of niacin twice per day.

"Too high of a dose of niacin can cause liver damage and high blood sugar levels, but too low of a dose does no good. The 500 mg. maximum dose per day seems to be just enough to be effective.

"There have been many lower extremities cut off because of diabetes, but I truly believe that if they had only given Jim-Niacin a chance I would have saved some of those limbs."

"Is there anyone else?" said B-12. "There it is folks, three powerful weapons to deal with this scourge diabetes. Now, for the final question of the evening, the question is what can we do to prevent extremely dry skin?"

"I'm Gina-Evening Primrose Oil, I'm an essential fatty acid and I'm one of the good oils that the body needs for beautiful skin. I recommend 1000-3000 mg. of evening primrose oil per day."

"I'm Jim-Niacin. In my view problems with dry skin, toe nail funguses, dandruff, and other skin problems is almost always a problem with blood circulation especially in the capillaries and small blood vessels.

"For extremely dry skin I recommend my unclogging dose of 250 mg. twice per day after a meal until the extremely dry skin condition has been cured, then throttle down to 250 mg. once a day for maintenance. But, be aware, most humans fear me, and for good reason, because my doses are no Sunday picnic or stroll through the park. My doses may heat up your skin like it is on fire and turn it as red as a beet.

"This flushing process is unpredictable, sometimes it will not happen at all, then other times it will last anywhere from five minutes to thirty minutes. It may not be pleasant, but it is my only way of unclogging the capillaries and small blood vessels," said Jim-Niacin.

"Is there anyone else?" said B-12. "What more could one ask for; those were two of the most powerful remedies that I ever heard of in dealing with a pesky humiliating dry skin condition.

"Remember, a dry skin problem is not something to be taken lightly, because you can see what is happening to the outer skin, but what's taking place inside with the vital organs could be a lot worse. "Citizens of Health-land Kingdom, that will end our town hall meeting for tonight, I would like to thank everyone for coming. Have a safe drive home," he said.

Chapter 6

Captain Fredrico was very impressed with the town hall meeting, especially learning how to deal with his long time dry skin problem and toe nail fungus. It had got to the point that he hated to take a shower.

It was bad enough struggling through the warmer months of the year, but the approach of winter was almost terrifying because a dry skin problem becomes much worse during the winter months. Much of the time during the winter he had to resort to what is called a bird bath by washing only his arm pits and private area. He had tried all kinds of oils, both internal and external. He had traveled on the super MD highway to the cure all metropolis, but all to no avail. Since the town hall meeting he had started off on Jim-Niacin's unclogging dose of 250 mg. of niacin twice a day after a meal.

The resulting benefits were obvious within a couple of days. Within days the treatment was so effective that the captain could barely wait to jump into the shower for the slightest reason. Also, within days his toe nails had started clearing and should be completely clear within a few months.

Also, in a few months the mayoral election will be taking place. Captain Fredrico felt very good about his chances of winning. According to the latest poll he had a four point lead.

That night as he and Jan were setting in the den watching TV, Captain Fredrico said, "You know, Jan, if I do become mayor of Healthland Kingdom I'm going to recognize Jim-Niacin by declaring a Jim-Niacin day."

"I know, dear, how much you love Jim-Niacin. He made it possible for you to be able to take regular showers again without you having to lotion down almost your whole body."
"I don't care how much he is

feared and misunderstood," said the Captain. "As far as I'm concerned Jim-Niacin is a miracle vitamin."

"I agree, my darling husband, about Jim-Niacin's abilities, if humans would just give him a chance he would save most of the lower extremities that are being lost because of Mr. Diabetes Disease."

The Captain got up from his recliner, walked over to Jan and gave her a warm tender kiss on her waiting luscious lips and said, "I'm off to bed, dear, I'll wait up for you."
"I won't be long, dear," said Jan.

Things had been rather calm in Health-land Kingdom for the last few months VC, VE, and John-pyridoxine all were very busy taking care of the town's population. About the only thing going on was the mayoral election coming up very soon.

They all thought the town hall meeting did a lot of good for the community. They felt it educated the citizens that there was a lot they could do for themselves concerning their health care.

That means that one will not
have   to jump on the super MD
highway for the slightest little pin prick
or minor inconvenience. Sure, there
is only so much we vitamins,
minerals, herbs, etc. can do to
promote health, we don't try to be
everything to everybody.
After the town hall meeting Mr.

Disease was steaming mad. He was even
thinking of calling a meeting of all the
different diseases. The nerve
of those vitamins, minerals, humans,
herbs and other nutrients trying to get
together and put him and his friends
out of business.

They want to try to put his most
successful friends like cancer,
diabetes, heart disease, and AIDS
out of business. He was not having
it; that was not going to be tolerated.
Mr. Disease started planning.

He would try to attack their left flank
by bringing back some of his old
friends like the Black Plague,
Tuberculosis, and West Nile, next he
would try to rush their right flank with
AIDS to try to split their force, then he

would try to rout them up the middle with lots of Cancer and Heart Disease.

I will take no prisoners. Who do they think this is, this is Mr. Disease and I don't play, I even quit school because they had recess. It is on. How dare they have this town hall meeting to try and get rid of me and my friends.

After a long hot summer the day of the mayoral election had finally arrived and it looked like it was going to be a big turn out. At seven o'clock p.m. Captain Fredrico, Jan, Bob, and Melinda had comfortable seats at election headquarters. All of the election precincts closed at seven o'clock p.m. sharp.

The captain and his family started watching the tally on the big electronic board as the precincts came in. Captain Fredrico jumped out to an early four point lead and was able to maintain the lead throughout the night as the precincts came in. Then, finally the election supervisor announced, "Citizens of Health-land Kingdom the mayor elect is Orry Fredrico." Within seconds several microphones were thrust in Captain Fredrico's face.

A reporter was almost yelling, "Captain Fredrico, how does it feel being the mayor elect of Health-land Kingdom."

"First, I would like to thank my family and all of the volunteers that worked so hard on my behalf to make this happen. Next, I would like to thank all of the citizens of Health-land Kingdom who had the faith and trust in me and backed it up by turning out to vote for me.

"Also, I would like to inform those that did not vote for me that I will be mayor of all the citizens of Health-land Kingdom. Finally, I would like to thank my opponent for a good clean hard fought campaign. Thanks again everyone. Good night."

Chapter 7

About one month after Captain Fredrico had been sworn in as mayor of Health-land Kingdom, he announced that the first Saturday in

March would be recognized by the town as Jim-Niacin's day.

On the morning of the first Saturday in March Mayor Fredrico stood at the podium at Healthy living park before a very large crowd.

"Citizens of Health-land Kingdom, today as your mayor I am proclaiming today as Jim-Niacin's day. We have on hand plenty of free food, drinks, and entertainment. To kick off this festive day, I'm going to deliver this short speech about the vitamin citizen we are celebrating today.

"Citizens of Health-land, Jim-Niacin is sort of an enigma. Many here had never heard of him, and of those that had, many of them fear and hate him. Still there is a great many that love this vitamin to death.

"I myself am one of those that dearly love Jim-Niacin and the good work he does. I am not telling you what I heard about Jim-Niacin, I'm telling you what I've personally experienced with my dealing with Jim-Niacin. I'm giving it to you first hand, straight from the horse's mouth.

"As I've told my wife and many others, I don't care what anyone says, to me Jim-Niacin is a miracle vitamin. This small, quiet, lowly member of the powerful B vitamin family is a Godsend as far as I'm concerned. As a proud virile human male I think of the many, many years that I suffered with extremely dry skin.

"For years I tried everything to get relief from this annoying dry skin condition. Even at the cure all metropolis they just prescribed an extremely expensive body cream that did little better than cheap over-the-counter lotions.

"Bathing and warm water had become the enemy. Washing only arm pits and the private area was becoming the norm, and I just hated my predicament. To me cleanliness is next to   Godliness.

"Sure, I had heard of Jim-Niacin, but it was mainly bad stuff, I never knew about his real power until I attended the town hall meeting. Over the years the dry skin problem was getting worse. Some type of fungus had invaded my toe nails and my skin was losing its luster in a few locations.

"The battle for healthy skin was a battle I knew I was losing , but no one could help me and I didn't know what to do. All of my life I've never been a quitter, I knew there was an answer, the problem was finding it, so I just kept on searching and searching.

"I was at my wits end, nothing or no one seemed able to help me find relief from my extremely dry skin condition. Then, at the final hour when all seemed lost and there was no hope left, Jim-Niacin came riding in on a big white horse at the town hall meeting.

"At the town hall meeting Jim-Niacin gave out his unclogging dose of 250 mg. twice a day after a meal. The first thing is I must warn you that taking Jim-Niacin's unclogging dose is no cake walk or stroll through the park. That is the reason many who have tried taking Jim's doses don't like him and is afraid of him.

"When Jim goes to work unclogging those capillaries and small blood vessels it is not pleasant by any means. This flushing process varies in intensity, sometimes it may be mild, then at other times your skin may feel like it is literally on fire.

"This flushing process may last anywhere from five to thirty minutes, but seldom lasts more than thirty minutes. I have no evidence to support this, but I believe diabetes itself is caused by a deficiency in niacin, chromium, and a few other nutrients.

"Citizens of Health-land I could go on and on praising Jim-Niacin because in the past he truly has been an unsung hero. I will add this and come to a close. Don't ever go over his maximum 500 mg. daily dose or it could cause liver damage.

"In closing, I will assure you that his unclogging dose got rid of my dandruff, dry skin, toe nail fungus, etc. Stand up Jim-Niacin and say a few words," concluded Captain Fredrico.

As Jim-Niacin arrived at the podium he stood tall and proud. The audience went wild with applause, then chanted, "We love you Jim, we love you Jim, we love you "Thank you, thank you, thank you," said Jim-Niacin, "and may God bless this great town and keep it healthy always."

THE END

Website: www.FLSirmans.com

**Blog:
http://www.freddiesirmansword.com**

www.ingramcontent.com/pod-product-compliance
Lightning Source LLC
Chambersburg PA
CBHW051727170526
45167CB00002B/839